THE LORD'S PRAYER

AUBREY COLEMAN

STUDY SUGGESTIONS

Thank you for choosing this study to help you dig into God's Word.
We are so passionate about men and women getting into Scripture, and we
are praying that this study will be a tool to help you do that.

HERE ARE A FEW TIPS TO HELP YOU GET THE MOST FROM THIS STUDY:

- Before you begin, take time to look into the context of the book. Find out who wrote it and learn about the cultural climate it was written in, as well as where it fits on the biblical timeline. Then take time to read through the entire book of the Bible we are studying if you are able. This will help you to get the big picture of the book and will aid in comprehension, interpretation, and application.

- Start your study time with prayer. Ask God to help you understand what you are reading and allow it to transform you (Psalm 119:18).

- Look into the context of the book as well as the specific passage.

- Before reading what is written in the study, read the assigned passage! Repetitive reading is one of the best ways to study God's Word. Read it several times, if you are able, before going on to the study. Read in several translations if you find it helpful.

- As you read the text, mark down observations and questions. Write down things that stand out to you, things that you notice, or things that you don't understand. Look up important words in a dictionary or interlinear Bible.

- Look for things like verbs, commands, and references to God. Notice key terms and themes throughout the passage.

- After you have worked through the text, read what is written in the study. Take time to look up any cross-references mentioned as you study.

- Then work through the questions provided in the book. Read and answer them prayerfully.

- Paraphrase or summarize the passage, or even just one verse from the passage. Putting it into your own words helps you to slow down and think through every word.

- Focus your heart on the character of God that you have seen in this passage. What do you learn about God from the passage you have studied? Adore Him and praise Him for who He is.

- Think and pray through application and how this passage should change you. Get specific with yourself. Resist the urge to apply the passage to others. Do you have sin to confess? How should this passage impact your attitude toward people or circumstances? Does the passage command you to do something? Do you need to trust Him for something in your life? How does the truth of the gospel impact your everyday life?

- We recommend you have a Bible, pen, highlighters, and journal as you work through this study. We recommend that ballpoint pens instead of gel pens be used in the study book to prevent smearing.

HERE ARE SEVERAL OTHER OPTIONAL RESOURCES THAT YOU MAY FIND HELPFUL AS YOU STUDY:

WWW.BLUELETTERBIBLE.ORG

This free website is a great resource for digging deeper. You can find translation comparison, an interlinear option to look at words in the original languages, Bible dictionaries, and even commentary.

A DICTIONARY

If looking up words in the Hebrew and Greek feels intimidating, look up words in English. Often times we assume we know the meaning of a word, but looking it up and seeing its definition can help us understand a passage better.

A DOUBLE-SPACED COPY OF THE TEXT

You can use a website like www.biblegateway.com to copy the text of a passage and print out a double-spaced copy to be able to mark on easily. Circle, underline, highlight, draw arrows, and mark in any way you would like to help you dig deeper and work through a passage.

TABLE OF CONTENTS

WEEK ONE

Day 1	08
Scripture Memory	29
Weekly Reflection	30

WEEK TWO

Day 1	32
Scripture Memory	53
Weekly Reflection	54

WEEK THREE

Day 1	56
Scripture Memory	77
Weekly Reflection	78

EXTRAS

Benedictions in Scripture	80
Petitions of the Lord's Prayer	82
31 Days of Prayer	83
What is the Gospel	85

OUR FATHER IN HEAVEN, YOUR
NAME BE HONORED AS HOLY.
YOUR KINGDOM COME,
YOUR WILL BE DONE ON EARTH
AS IT IS IN HEAVEN.

GIVE US TODAY OUR DAILY
BREAD. AND FORGIVE US OUR
DEBTS, AS WE ALSO HAVE
FORGIVEN OUR DEBTORS.

AND DO NOT BRING US INTO
TEMPTATION, BUT DELIVER
US FROM THE EVIL ONE.

MATTHEW 6:9-13

WEEK ONE

DAY 1

INTRODUCTION

Read Matthew 6:5-13

"Jesus Christ, the Son of God, has made a way for us to commune with God in prayer."

It is a privilege as Christians to approach the Father in prayer. Prayer is more than a conversation with God; it is sacred communion with God that is seen in the story of Scripture from beginning to end. Communing with God in prayer means drawing near to God, sitting in His presence, and coming to Him for help and comfort when we need it. Jesus Christ, the Son of God, has made a way for us to commune with God in prayer. Even when we do not know what to pray, we are empowered by the Holy Spirit to pray as we ought. Scripture is saturated with the power and privilege of prayer. We are not only privileged to pray, but we are also commanded to pray. Prayer is an active work of adoring God, confessing to God, thanking God, and making requests to God. As we are assured of its necessity as Christians, the Lord's Prayer gives powerful insight into what our prayer lives should look like.

The Lord's Prayer is one of the most recited and shared passages of Scripture among Christians. This prayer has been rightfully held in reverence since it was first spoken by our Lord Jesus Himself. Jesus shared this rich prayer with his disciples as a means of teaching, correcting, and modeling to them the important elements of prayer.

In considering the Lord's Prayer, we should recognize the purpose for which it was given. While it is certainly right and fitting to pray the prayer as it was originally recorded in the New Testament, especially as it helps us to think more intentionally about what we are saying when we pray, it does not seem that Jesus gave us this prayer only to recite. Instead, the primary intent seems to give us a model for how we are to structure and organize our prayers. We draw this conclusion from the fact that in the two times the prayer was recorded, it was not recorded in the same exact way, but with the same principle.

The Lord's Prayer is recorded twice in the Gospels. We find the shorter version of the prayer in Luke 11 and the longer version of the prayer in Matthew 6. As we continue through this study, we will focus primarily on the passage in the Gospel of Matthew with some reference to the passage in the Gospel of Luke and other supporting passages in the Bible.

Entering into Matthew, we find the Lord's Prayer right in the middle of the Sermon on the Mount (Matthew 5-7). This sermon is given to explain that Jesus demands a righteousness that exceeds that of the scribes and the Pharisees (Matthew 5:27-28). Jesus makes it clear that he did not die for good appearances, but for lives that would be transformed by the power of the gospel.

> Jesus came to give us a righteousness that works its way into the depth of our hearts and changes our attitudes.

The Sermon on the Mount was a prominent message during a time when the original teachings of the Law (the compilation of decrees found in the first five books of the Bible) had become corrupted over time.

As these teachings carried into the New Testament, Jesus saw that the Law had been viewed in a ritualistic and habitual way. Instead, Jesus lays a foundational understanding of the way the law should be viewed (Matthew 5:17-20). The Law is the standard set before us by God to obey perfectly so that we might have a right relationship with Him. Evidenced in the history of Scripture and even now, we do not perfectly obey. Therefore, Jesus came to make a way for us to have a right relationship with God. He came to fulfill the law for all who would put their faith and trust in Him as their Savior. Because of this, we view the law differently—we obey out of love and hope in Jesus, rather than out of obligation.

We are reminded from the context of these chapters that our actions should not flow from a ritualistic pattern, but rather our actions should be an overflow of our hearts of faith to walk in a manner worthy of the gospel at work in us. This perfectly prefaces the Lord's Prayer. There might be a temptation to approach prayer in a way that is ritualistic or outwardly pleasing, with the desires of our hearts and our attitude towards these practices unchanged. We might even pray without a true understanding of what our words mean or why we are even praying them.

Therefore, Jesus provides a rich foundational theology for prayer by presenting the strong example of the Lord's Prayer right in the middle of His corrective teaching. He reminds His disciples of how we should pray. No one is better able to teach us these valuable elements and the true nature of prayer than Jesus Himself.

As we dive into the teaching of the Lord's Prayer, let us be expectant of what God will teach us about Himself and how we are called to worship Him in prayer.

1. What is your initial understanding of prayer?

2. How have you seen or heard the Lord's Prayer used?

3. Read through Matthew 6:5-13. What line of the prayer stands out to you the most and why? What questions do you have about it?

4. Write down a prayer asking for God's help as you begin to study the Lord's Prayer.

IT MATTERS HOW WE PRAY

WEEK ONE

DAY 2

IT MATTERS HOW WE PRAY

Read Luke 11:1

"Prayer is an overflow of what we believe in our hearts."

In Luke 11, we see Jesus separated from His disciples and praying alone. Upon returning to the disciples, they eagerly insist, "Lord, teach us how to pray." Jesus was praying in such a way that challenged their understanding of prayer and they humbly asked for instruction. Notice, the disciples do not ask him to teach them *what* to pray. There is a clear distinction in how the disciples were asking for guidance. They desired more of an outline or guiding principle for prayer, rather than precise and set words and phrases. The disciples were seeking an authentic and conversational prayer life with God in the same way they had seen and witnessed in Jesus' prayer life. The fact that Jesus answers this request with the Lord's Prayer implies that it matters how we pray.

How we pray reveals our true thoughts and beliefs about God. Prayer is an overflow of what we believe in our hearts. Therefore, the way in which we do so says a lot about who we actually think He is. If we are praying for God's help, we reveal an understanding of His power and authority. If we are repenting of sin to God in prayer, we recognize Him as the One who made a way for forgiveness and righteousness. If we approach Him with our burdens, we acknowledge His capability to carry the weight of them all. Everything we pray about, speaks of our fundamental belief of who we believe God is.

In the same way, our prayers speak of how we view ourselves and others. Prayer reveals how we view ourselves in relation to God. We reveal what we believe we are capable of on our own when we neglect to pray for certain things. We share our desires and hopes and fears and doubts in our prayers. We learn a lot about ourselves and what we value most when we consider how and what we pray. Prayer exposes our hearts. We pray about the things that matter to us (Matthew 6:25-32, Matthew 6:33, Matthew 22:37-40). We pray about the things we care about. Consider your most frequented prayer request and what that tells you about your priorities. Our lives of prayer speak more of our hearts than we may have ever realized. This is why Jesus is giving such an emphasis on how. If the words are bountiful and beautiful, but our hearts are unchanged, what is the intention of our prayers? If we are highly revered and celebrated for our prayers by others, but we have no concern for how God views them, what does it matter? Jesus has made a way for us to pray that pleases God and therefore His direction and guidance on what prayer should look like holds insurmountable value.

The beauty of the Lord's Prayer is that it teaches us to pray as we ought. It guides and shapes our understanding of God's desires for us to approach Him in prayer with changed hearts.

1. Consider your prayer life. In what ways do you see a need for growth or greater understanding?

2. How does your prayer life reveal what you believe about God?

3. What does your prayer life reveal about what you prioritize?

4. If every prayer you ever prayed was answered, what would you realize you should be praying more fervently about?

HOW NOT TO PRAY

WEEK ONE

DAY 3

HOW NOT TO PRAY

PART 1

Read Matthew 6:5-6

"While they seemed to be praying with postures towards God, they were only focused on themselves. They desired to be seen by man, rather than to be seen by God."

Before Jesus teaches us how to pray, He starts with how not to pray. We should take these instructions seriously because they give boundaries to how we can honor God and worship Him properly in prayer. He gives fundamental understanding in the Sermon on the Mount about how our hearts are to be changed so that our actions are changed too.

Here in Matthew 6:5, Jesus starts with the actions of the hypocrites to reveal the deeper substance of their hearts. Hypocrisy in the New Testament is drawn from the culture of that day and age. A hypocrite was one who engaged in play-acting, drama, and theater. The implication is made that some were approaching prayer in a performance-based way. He is speaking to those who went about prayer in a way that was externally righteous, but internally insincere. Their prayers were not truly genuine, but rather a dutiful act, to make a visually pleasing display to others.

There were two main places where a Jew in Jesus' day might pray hypocritically. They might pray at the synagogue at the time of public prayer or on the street at the appointed times of prayer. Praying in the churches was a normal place for prayer. However, it was not the typical place for private and personal prayer. The street corners were places of public notice, where one was easily seen. Again, not a usual place for personal and private prayer. If these places are being addressed, it is evident that they were revisited by the scribes and Pharisees often and likely more so than they frequented quiet rooms with closed doors for a personal time of prayer. The scribes and Pharisees were calling attention to themselves in the public eye as they prayed while likely neglecting the hidden, quiet times of prayer.

In all their exercises of devotion, Jesus warns them against the desire to be commended by their neighbors and making much of themselves. While they seemed to be praying with postures towards God, they were only focused on themselves. They desired to be seen by man, rather than to be seen by God. Jesus is clear. Those who pray in such a way will have their longed-for reward. They will be seen by others and likely be celebrated for it. But that reward will end with their time on earth. The outward show will fade away with their earthly bodies.

Ultimately, Jesus is encouraging Christians to look at their hearts. He is asking us to rid ourselves of hypocrisy. If our public display of prayer is not an authentic reflection of our private time in prayer, we are not praying in the way God intended us to. We are making prayer about us, instead of reverent communication with the God of the universe. The reward that comes from God is incomparably better than that which comes from people. Let not the desire for approval from others distort the privilege of prayer. A holy God now finds you as one approved in Christ Jesus. May our prayers reflect an unbending devotion to the only One whose approval truly matters in light of eternity.

> **JESUS IS ENCOURAGING CHRISTIANS TO LOOK AT THEIR HEARTS. HE IS ASKING US TO RID OURSELVES OF HYPOCRISY.**

1. Jesus gives examples of how we should not pray and He begins with the hypocrites in Matthew 6:5. How were people being hypocritical in their prayers? How did Jesus warn against this in Matthew 6:1-4?

2. What application is given to the hypocrites in verse 6?

3. Consider your prayer life behind closed doors. How might it look different when surrounded by people? How does this Scripture challenge the intentions of our hearts in both public and private prayer?

WEEK ONE

DAY 4

HOW NOT TO PRAY

PART 2

Read Matthew 6:7-8

"He knows the reality of our hearts, even when our words do not honestly express them in prayer."

The second way Jesus instructs us not to pray is like the Gentiles. The Gentiles approached prayer in a way that was full of tradition and repetition that often became convoluted with words and little meaning. Jesus reasserts us to consider the condition of our hearts in prayer in another way, "When you pray, do not heap up empty phrases as the Gentiles do, for they think that they will be heard for their many words. Do not be like them, for your Father knows what you need before you ask him." (Matthew 6:7–8)

We can understand why Jesus is aiming to pull us away from using empty and meaningless words in prayer. Because of our sinful nature, we are prone to wander especially in prayer. Think of times when you began to pray and drifted off in your mind to think about other things. Consider times when you began praying in a group and forgot what you had even said after finishing with an "Amen." We can become so aware of phrases and verbiage in prayer that we know what to say and how to say it in such a way that puts us in an auto-pilot mode for prayer. But God is not fooled. Jesus warns us not to heap up empty phrases thinking we will be heard by God. He knows the reality of our hearts, even when our words do not honestly express them in prayer.

Notice Jesus does not say if you pray, but when you pray. In Christ, we are given the freedom to come to God as we are. He does not ask that we attain a lofty vocabulary or profound understanding in the ways of prayer. He asks, simply, that we approach Him in the way that Jesus instructs us to in Scripture. We are set free from the need to impress God. Jesus has already given us the most impressive stance before God by His own life, death, and resurrection. In Christ, we are invited into God's family as children. We can approach him closely and honestly as our Father who knows all about us.

This does not negate the need to approach God with reverence. Simple language does not mean careless petitions. The expression of this prayer directs our hearts to be fully reverent to God's power, fully vowed to God's work, and fully dependent on Him for all things. We are called to pray with hearts that have been softened from stone through the mighty and astounding work of Jesus Christ at work in us.

As we discussed before, how we pray says a lot about how we view God. Do we believe he knows our needs before we ask? Do we assume we must reach Him with impressive words or do we trust in the access we have gained fully through faith in Christ Jesus? Do we believe he is distant or near? Do we believe He is gracious and kind, sovereign and good? As Christians, we can pray differently than those in the world. We pray with knowledge and wisdom from God's Word. We pray with hope and confidence in the gift of grace offered to us in the finished work of Christ Jesus. We are free from approaching God with a need to earn His favor. Rather, we pray with close familiarity as children of God, knowing our Father knows our needs before we even ask them. In fact, He knows our needs better than we do and He is more committed to meeting them in the deepest and most lasting way.

> We are called to pray with hearts that have been softened from stone through the mighty and astounding work of Jesus Christ at work in us.

1. Prayer is intended to engage your heart and mind. What does it look like to engage your heart and mind in prayer?

2. How does understanding God's knowledge of you free you to come to Him as you are in prayer?

3. How is the Lord's Prayer simple, yet without simple meaning?

PRAY THEN LIKE THIS

WEEK ONE

DAY 5

PRAY THEN LIKE THIS

Read Matthew 6:9

We first learn to pray by seeing others pray. When we are new believers and unfamiliar with how to pray, we may find ourselves watching others who pray confidently and biblically. By surrounding ourselves with praying people, we witness the power of prayer and grow in our practice of prayer. When learning how to pray and even if stumbling and fumbling through it, growth is happening. There are many practical tips and even acronyms to help us model our prayers. But we truly learn to pray best by praying ourselves and listening to others pray. This is very similar to what Jesus does for His disciples. Instead of giving them a list of rules for prayers, he models prayer for them. The model of this prayer gives us a reference point when we feel unsure about how to pray. It even gives us a place to return to when we feel we have lost our way in prayer.

It is important to consider the layout of this prayer that Jesus modeled. The Lord's Prayer includes six petitions. Initially, our focus is outside of ourselves with eyes fixed on God. We are to acknowledge Him for who He is and set our hearts on His eternal purposes, even when thinking of our present-day circumstances.

> All of the first three requests have to do with the glory of God being made known—the central goal of the Christian life.

We are called to pray for God's name to be honored, for His kingdom to come, and for His will to be done here on earth.

> The last three requests concentrate on our personal needs, whether physical, relational or spiritual.

Notice the order of the layout: God and his kingdom are appropriately placed first, then the needs of man follow. This how we are called to come to the Lord in prayer. We do not start by asking for all of our needs and making our requests to Him. Instead, we posture ourselves in humble reverence, acknowledging Him for Who He is

WEEK 1 DAY 5 | 25

and praising His name. His glory is due before our wants are presented. This is a strong parallel to the Ten Commandments and how they were ordered: the first four having to do with God's glory and the last six having to do with how those who are God's people should live among others. Only when God has been given His proper place will all other things fall into their proper places.

Our hearts are naturally inclined towards ourselves. It is only by the transforming power of the gospel, enabled by the work of the Holy Spirit, that our hearts are turned towards God. Because of this, prayer must be a continual practice of our faith in our daily lives. The more we pray, the more it becomes ingrained in the way we live. The more we are giving ourselves to prayer, the more we see our need for God's astounding provision.

> ONLY WHEN GOD HAS BEEN GIVEN HIS PROPER PLACE WILL ALL OTHER THINGS FALL INTO THEIR PROPER PLACES.

1. How do you typically structure your prayers? Are they focused on God or yourself?

2. How do your prayers reflect the desires of your heart?

3. Why is it important that you acknowledge God's glory first in prayer?

BUT WHEN YOU PRAY, GO INTO YOUR PRIVATE ROOM, SHUT YOUR DOOR, AND PRAY TO YOUR FATHER WHO IS IN SECRET. AND YOUR FATHER WHO SEES IN SECRET WILL REWARD YOU.

MATTHEW 6:6

WEEKLY REFLECTION

Week One: Matthew 6:5-13; Luke 11:1

Paraphrase the passages from this week.

What did you observe from this week's text about God and His character?

What do these passages teach about the condition of mankind and about yourself?

How do these passage point to the gospel?

How should you respond to these passages? What is the personal application?

What specific action steps can you take this week to apply these passages?

OUR FATHER

WEEK TWO

DAY 1

OUR FATHER

Review Matthew 6:5-13

Read Matthew 6:9,
John 1:12-13,
Ephesians 2:18-19

"We are adopted as sons and daughters and heirs with Christ."

At times, prayer may seem like a daunting task. We read local news articles bringing words to injustice, suffering, starvation, destruction, and sin all around the world. We may question where to even begin in prayer. But Jesus gives us a simple answer—begin in prayer by remembering Who you are praying to. God is teaching us through Jesus how He wants His people to approach Him. He intentionally draws our hearts and minds not to the circumstances surrounding us or needs to be presented, but He purposefully draws our attention to Himself with the words, "Our Father."

We may often approach prayer in a very personal way, "My Father in heaven…" There is a great deal of importance to consider in the fact that we do not begin this prayer with *my*, but *our*. One changed pronoun reminds us that we are not alone. This is a small, yet strong challenge to consider your relationship with God as not only personal but communal with other Christians. When we enter into a relationship with God, we enter into a relationship with God's people.

In Christ, we gain access to God as His children. We are adopted as sons and daughters and heirs with Christ. In prayer, we have the opportunity to approach God as representatives of His family. God is at work to further His kingdom through all of His people. Beginning our prayers with "Our Father" portrays a greater understanding of our responsibility as His children and challenges our individualistic views of prayer. Our communal posture in prayer reminds us that walking faithfully as a Christian is intended to be in the context of other Christians. Even as we pray alone, we are called to pray with a heart for Christ's church and eyes fixed on His greater kingdom purposes.

The name of God used in this prayer is Father. Although the work of prayer is a fully trinitarian work, we are to direct our prayers to the Father. The Son of God serves as our mediator in prayer (1 Timothy 2:5), the Spirit of God helps us to pray as we ought (Romans 8:26), but we are to address our prayers to God the Father. What a gracious gift that we can address a holy God in such a familial way. It is only through the saving work of Christ, that we are offered access to God in a personal and intimate way (John 14:6). Jesus Christ made a way for us to enter into the family of God—no longer as orphans or strangers, but brought near as children of God. The privilege to come to God as Father is only given to those who have placed their faith in Jesus Christ. Those who reject Jesus as their Lord and Savior cannot call Him Father because they are not part of the family (John 1:9–13).

> We can trust Him as our Protector and Provider, with secured hope in Him to satisfy all of our needs.

1. When we come to know Christ as our Lord and Savior, we are brought into the family of God. How can you pray with and for others in light of this reality?

2. How does praying with communal understanding bring the kingdom purposes of God to a focus?

3. How do you have access to draw near to God as Father?

4. How does addressing God as Father posture your heart towards Him?

IN HEAVEN

WEEK TWO

DAY 2

IN HEAVEN

Read Matthew 6:9,
Psalm 103:19,
Psalm 115:3,
Isaiah 66:1

> "Understanding that He is in heaven deepens our praise and humbles us. It leads us to approach Him with familiarity and awe-stricken wonder all the same."

The Lord's Prayer is filled with small phrases of rich truth when we take notice of them. Jesus is intentional with His words, each drawing our focus to the greater hope of who God is in prayer. The next phrase in the prayer is "in heaven." When Jesus refers to His Father who is in heaven, He is not speaking only of a place, but of God's heavenly character.

One attribute this phrase points to is God's heavenly perfection. Heaven is the perfect dwelling place, so when God the Father is described as being in heaven, it implies His perfection. Jesus describes His Father earlier in the Sermon on the Mount as heavenly when referring to His perfection (Matthew 5:48). Just as understanding His fatherhood draws us near, His attribute of perfection places us in proper reverence. Understanding that He is in heaven deepens our praise and humbles us. It leads us to approach Him with familiarity and awe-stricken wonder all the same. His perfection exalts His Fatherhood, freed from any earthly weakness, restraint, or flaw, and leads us to His perfect love for us as His children. In His perfect nature, God is exalted above the earth, and He is not like us. This brings unending comfort to know we are not seeking help from those who dwell upon this earth, those confined by time, space, or physical limits, but from One who inhabits the heavenly realms.

Another attribute highlighted in this phrase is God's transcendence. God's attribute of transcendence is closely related to His sovereignty. Being transcendent means that God is above all. He is beyond our experience, even beyond our categories and our understanding. Ephesians 4:6 says that God is "one God and Father of all, who is over all and through all and in all." The transcendent nature of God gives a bigger picture of how He relates to His creation. He is distinctly different from all that He creates. He is not like anything we have ever known. He is beyond our unfathomable mind. He is higher than every aspect of His creation. He is the only one like Him (Jeremiah 10:6). The transcendence of God is woven throughout the Bible from start to finish. He has no beginning and no end. In seeking to understand this attribute, we are all the more humbled and He is all the more exalted. Jesus shows us in this model of prayer that as we come to God in prayer as His children, we are also coming to the almighty God of the universe.

However, in His perfect and transcendent nature, we must understand that God is not far off. He is intimately involved with all of creation. It is miraculous to consider the implications of this. God is approachable and near to us! He does not leave us to govern ourselves or to control our own lives. God is seated on His throne in heaven and rules over all things. He works in all things to the greater good of His people and to the glory of His name. He is trustworthy in the fact that He sees all, knows all, and is all. Hope in the sovereign rule of God shapes our prayers to align with His wants. His vantage point is beyond what we can see or know! We find rest and comfort in God's attributes, approaching Him in prayer with an understanding of His perfect and transcendent nature, and trusting in His sovereign rule.

> He is trustworthy in the fact that He sees all, knows all, and is all. Hope in the sovereign rule of God shapes our prayers to align with His wants.

1. Summarize what you have learned about God's attribute of heavenly perfection.

2. Summarize your understanding of God's attribute of transcendence.

3. How does acknowledging God's perfection and sovereignty shape your response to the way He answers your prayers?

YOUR NAME BE HONORED AS HOLY

WEEK TWO

DAY 3

YOUR NAME BE HONORED AS HOLY

Read Matthew 6:9,
Psalm 113:2-3,
Psalm 57:5,
Psalm 69:34

You have likely heard of a petition before. It is a piece of paper that people pass around for others to sign in hopes that it will serve as written evidence of an agreement on some issue. A petition is a request. Jesus gave His disciples in the Lord's Prayer specific requests known as petitions. These are the things that Jesus specifies His disciples should ask for in their prayers. The first thing that Jesus tells them to pray for is that the name of God would be holy (or some translations use the word hallowed). This means that His name is to be sacred and set apart. This word is only applicable to God because He is sacred and set apart from every created thing. There is none holy like the Lord and there is none like Him (1 Samuel 2:2)

The holiness of God is one of His most profound attributes. In his book, *The Knowledge of the Holy*, A. W. Tozer writes,

> *Holy is the way God is. To be holy He does not conform to a standard. He is that standard. He is holy with an infinite, incomprehensible fullness of purity that is incapable of being other than it is. Because He is holy, His attributes are holy. That is, whatever we think of as belonging to God must be thought of as holy.*

Not only is God holy in his actions, but He is also holy in His essence. All that He is and does is holy.

Because of God's holiness and our sinful nature, we have no right or merit to approach Him. In Christ, we have remarkable and unexplainable hope. Romans 6:23 says, "For the wages of sin is death, but the gift of God is eternal life in Jesus Christ our Lord." Our sin has separated us from God and even in our most righteous efforts, we could never attain the holiness required to draw near to a holy God. Our sin earns us death, separation from God in an earthly and eternal sense. But in His grace and mercy, God sent His only Son to obtain righteousness for us by living perfectly among us. In His perfection, Jesus Christ could stand in our place on the cross to take the punishment that we deserved. Putting our faith in Christ as our Lord and Savior, we acknowledge the punishment we deserve, repenting of our ways, and giving our lives fully to the purposes of God. Through salvation, Christ bridges the gap between our sin and God's holiness. We have undeserved access to God in prayer. An appropriate response to this great gift is awe and worship.

What Jesus is calling us to in prayer is to worship God in His holiness. It means approaching God in prayer with the right understanding. It means revering Him with absolute reverence and humility. It means considering His holy grandeur with every word, request, and thought in prayer. But Jesus is not asking us to do this only on a personal level. Personal praise is vital to our prayer life, but bringing glory to God goes beyond us. In prayer, our hearts are to be stirred for all people to know and revere God as holy, to worship and praise His name and to enjoy Him now and forevermore. We are to pray for God to act in the hearts of all who do not revere Him as holy so that He will receive the honor and glory due His Name.

When we lift up our hearts in prayer, we are to cry out, "Father, may the whole world worship and praise You!" God's glory far surpasses our personal adoration for Him. So, our hope is that all would adore and praise God with ringing resound. May God's name be honored as holy among the stars and the heavens and every living creature on earth. May God's name be honored as holy from the highest of the mountain tops to the deepest depths of the sea. May God's name be honored as holy amidst trial, suffering, and every kind of evil. May God's name be honored as holy during every celebration, blessing, and every kind of gift. In every crevice and facet of the cosmos, may God's name be honored as holy. This is to be our prayer.

> In prayer, our hearts are to be stirred for all people to know and revere God as holy, to worship and praise His name and to enjoy Him now and forevermore.

1. In Christ, we have gained access to approach a holy God. How should you approach Him as such in prayer?

2. How can you pray to view God as holy? How should you pray for the spreading of the gospel to reach all people of the earth so that they too can see Him as holy?

3. Summarize God's attribute of holiness.

YOUR KINGDOM COME

WEEK TWO

DAY 4

YOUR KINGDOM COME

Read Matthew 6:10,
Psalm 47:2,
Colossians 1:13,
Psalm 22:27-28,
Isaiah 45:22-24

God is altogether holy, splendorous, magnificent, glorious and worthy of all the world's praise and adoration. Yet all on earth have not revered God as holy. We see this in the ways of the world—war and tragedy happen all around us, oppression is unceasing, hunger for power and wealth are sought for at all costs, disunity, corruption, and all kinds of evil speak against God's holy order. We pray for all people to be brought out of the darkness and into the light, to bring worship due God's name. And yet, we pray with a promise. God promises a day where every single knee will bow and every tongue will confess the righteousness of God. The second petition transitions seamlessly from a recognition of the worship due His name to praying for God's kingdom to come when God's holy order and rule will be fully restored.

During Jesus' earthly ministry he spoke often about the kingdom of God. We are told in Matthew 24:14, that "This good news of the kingdom will be proclaimed in all the world as a testimony to all nations, and then the end will come." He also reminds us to make it our earthly pursuit to, "seek first the kingdom of God" (Matthew 6:33).

So, what is this kingdom he is referring to? The kingdom of God can be defined as God's people gathered together under God's rule and blessing. Praying for God's kingdom to come, means praying for His good and perfect rule. It means seating Christ on His rightful throne in our hearts as the sovereign King and praying for the final establishment of His kingdom to come. We see a glimpse of this coming kingdom in Matthew 25:31-34,

> *When the Son of Man comes in his glory, and all the angels with him, then he will sit on his glorious throne. All the nations will be gathered before him, and he will separate them one from another, just as a shepherd separates the sheep from the goats. He will put the sheep on his right and the goats on the left. Then the king will say to those on his right, 'Come, you who are blessed by my Father; inherit the kingdom prepared for you from the foundation of the world.*

When we pray, "Your kingdom come," we are praying for Christ to return as King of kings and Lord of lords (Revelation 19:16) to establish His kingdom on earth and rule forevermore. We are praying for Him to gather all of His people together; from every tongue and tribe, every people group and nation, all of God's redeemed. On a more immediate level, we pray for God to rule in our hearts. We are asking for His kingship in our lives. We may be tempted to build our own little kingdoms here on earth of comfort, approval, possessions, and wealth. But, the only lasting kingdom is the kingdom to come.

Our prayers must be shaped by the reality that earth is not our end. We can pray for healing, for safety, for opportunities, for the desires of our hearts, for specific happenings and the like, but our hope is not in God answering in the way we ask. Praying for God's kingdom to come, reminds us that our present circumstances are not eternal and that no earthly gain apart from Christ is lasting. Our ultimate aim in our petitions should not be to make earth more comfortable or to establish a home for us in the world. Instead, the heartbeat of our prayers should beat, not for the temporary, but for the eternal hope to come. Our hope is that God has promised His kingdom will come and all who revere Him will enter in.

ON A MORE IMMEDIATE LEVEL, WE PRAY FOR GOD TO RULE IN OUR HEARTS.

1. Read the Scriptures for today. List what God's kingdom is like.

2. What does it look like for your prayers to be shaped by the reality that earth is not your end, believing your true citizenship is in heaven?

3. How does the promise of God's kingdom bring comfort to you in prayer?

YOUR WILL BE DONE

WEEK TWO

DAY 5

48

YOUR WILL BE DONE ON EARTH AS IT IS IN HEAVEN

Read Matthew 6:10,
Psalm 143:10,
1 John 5:14,
James 4:13-15

"In prayer, our ultimate desire should be that God's will accomplishes God's purposes and brings fulfillment to God's glorious plan of redemption."

Prayer is the communal work of God's people for God's purposes. We see this threaded into the teaching of the Lord's Prayer. Understanding God rightly and reverently leads us to pray as we ought. Jesus instructs His disciples to the third petition for God's will to be done on earth as it is in heaven. Asking for God's will to be done is an acknowledgment that God knows what's best. It is putting hope and faith in His good and perfect will and surrendering ourselves to it.

When we properly honor God and seat Him on the throne of our hearts, His desires become our desires. God's will becomes that which we seek after. This does not mean that we will always understand God's intentions or adhere to His plan without pain and confusion. We witness Jesus Christ, himself, praying in anguish in the garden of Gethsemane. After His betrayal, He knew the hour had come for his arrest and ultimately His death. He prayed three different times, "My Father, if it is possible, let this cup pass from me. Yet not as I will, but as you will." Jesus was deeply grieved by the task before Him, and yet His prayers possessed a greater hope in the perfect care of His Father.

Our vantage point is flawed. We make plans and see only minimally how they might affect our lives. But God has an aerial view of the trajectory of our lives. He sees the inner-working of every choice we make and every path we take. He knows all things before they even come to be. With a grand and all-encompassing perspective, He can promise to work all things together for the good of those who love Him. All things that were made, were made by Him. There is nothing on this earth made apart from God. That is why we confidently trust in His good and perfect will and pray for it to be done.

In prayer, our ultimate desire should be that God's will accomplishes God's purposes and brings fulfillment to God's glorious plan of redemption. We know that God wants to prepare us, shape us, and sanctify us. He

WEEK 2 DAY 5

wants to prepare us for heaven. We pray for His will to be done on earth as it is in heaven because we know eternity with God is the ultimate reward of the Christian. God's will in heaven is perfect and complete. Amid our prayers, may we plead for God's will to be done. Even when we can't fully understand or struggle to see what God is doing, may we ask God to prepare our hearts to receive His will with hope and confidence, knowing that He is sovereign overall.

YOUR WILL BE DONE ON EARTH AS IT IS IN HEAVEN.

1. How do you see a need to surrender your will to God's will in prayer?

2. What hope do you have in God's kingdom to come?

3. What comfort in prayer do you draw from the reality that God's will is perfect and complete in heaven?

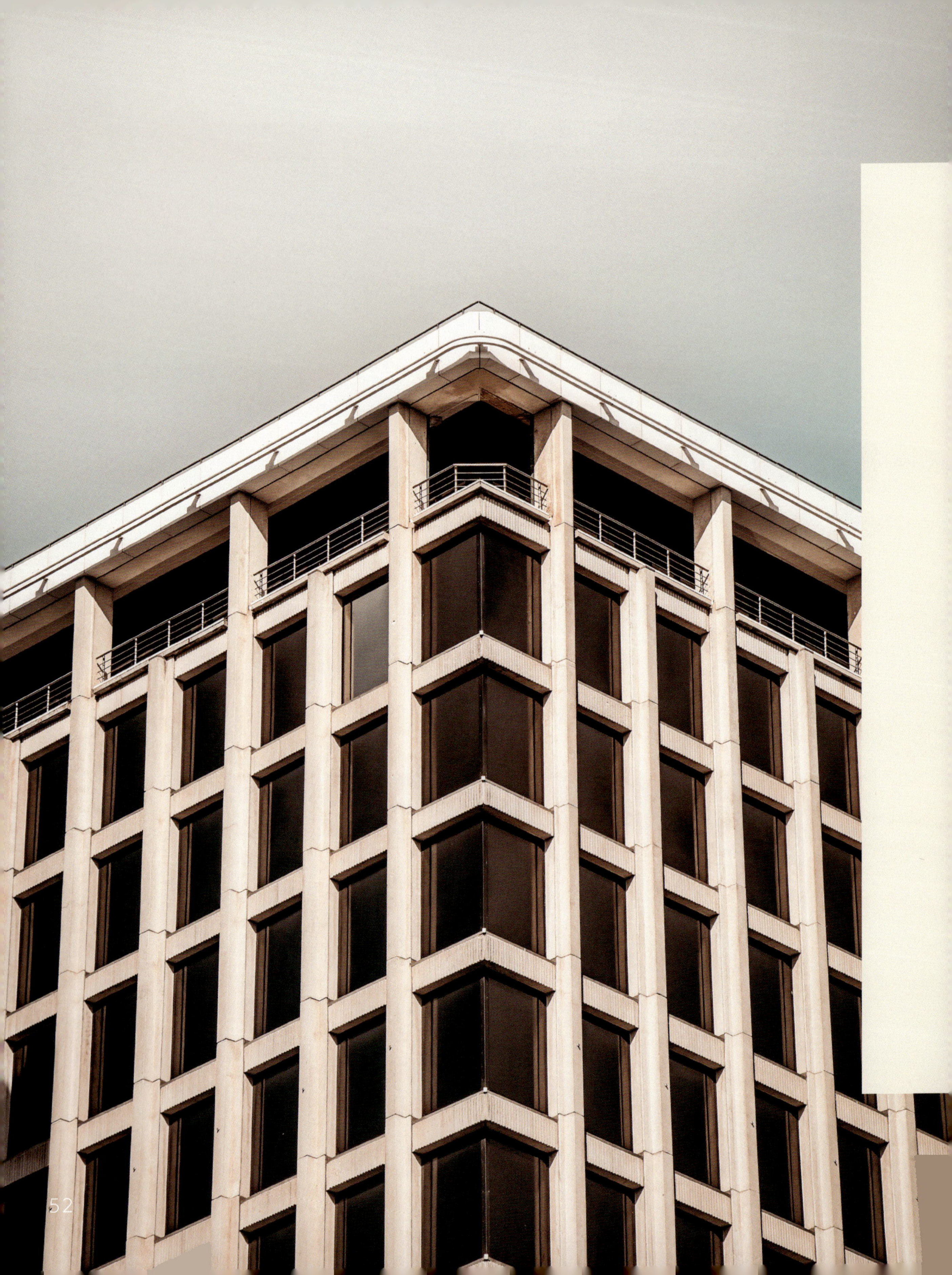

THEREFORE, YOU SHOULD PRAY LIKE THIS: OUR FATHER IN HEAVEN, YOUR NAME BE HONORED AS HOLY. YOUR KINGDOM COME. YOUR WILL BE DONE ON EARTH AS IT IS IN HEAVEN.

MATTHEW 6:9-10

WEEKLY REFLECTION

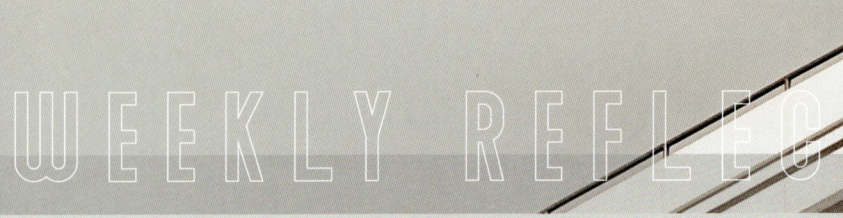

Week Two: Review all passages from the week

Paraphrase the passages from this week.

What did you observe from this week's text about God and His character?

What do these passages teach about the condition of mankind and about yourself?

How do these passage point to the gospel?

How should you respond to these passages? What is the personal application?

What specific action steps can you take this week to apply these passages?

GIVE US TODAY OUR DAILY BREAD

WEEK THREE

DAY 1

GIVE US TODAY OUR DAILY BREAD

Review Matthew 6:5-13

Read Matthew 6:11,
Philippians 4:19,
Proverbs 30:8-9,
Matthew 5:6,
John 6:35,
John 5:47-51

"We are needy creatures in need of the provision and care of our Creator."

Leading up to this fourth petition, the Lord's Prayer has focused intentionally on the character of God. We see the need to acknowledge God's fatherhood, God's transcendent and sovereign attributes, God's holiness, and God's perfect will and reign. After bringing to light the truth of God's character, Jesus then points us to consider our needs in prayer. We are not like God. We are not self-created, self-existing, self-sufficient, or self-dependent. We are needy creatures in need of the provision and care of our Creator. It is miraculous to consider that from the moment God creates life inside a mother's womb, its survival is dependent on the sustaining power of God. Even after birth, our lives are dependent on God supplying our every need.

Consider all of the things you need daily to survive. We are not sufficient on our own. We are incapable of providing for ourselves in the way that God can provide for us. We see this simply in our daily need for food. Without it, our bodies grow weak, we lose energy and eventually we cannot live without it. The fourth petition begins our personal requests in prayer. It reminds us of our utter dependence on God for even the most basic needs of life.

Jesus teaches us to pray that God would give us daily bread (Matthew 6:11). This is not just a request for daily food, but even more so daily provision and nourishment from the Bread of Life (John 6:35). In John 6, Jesus is teaching the crowd that physical provision is given by God, and although significant, there is a spiritual provision that endures to eternal life (John 6:27). There is bread that does not rot or spoil, but instead nourishes sustaining life in us that continues forever.

Jesus uses the example of the Israelites in the wilderness to remind the crowd that physical bread is not enough. Life in the wilderness was hard, and soon the people began to complain that it would be better to be back in Egypt, where they had a plentiful amount of food to eat. In response to these complaints, God promised to "rain bread from heaven" (Exodus 16:4). The next morning, the Israelites found "fine flakes on the desert surface, as fine as frost on the ground. It resembled coriander seed, was white and tasted like wafers made with honey." (Exodus 6:14, 31). When God miraculously provided for His people, He did so by giving them physical bread and reminding them of their ultimate dependence on Him.

We physically need food, and spiritually, we need God. The physical substance will help us temporarily, but the spiritual substance will last forever. Jesus is teaching us in this petition of the Lord's Prayer to approach God in prayer with humble dependence, asking Him to provide what we need and to sustain us from day to day, both physically and spiritually. We do not need great and frivolous riches, but we can come before God and ask Him for what we need, trusting that He will always give us whatever is required for life and godliness. This looks like asking God for daily provision, enough food to eat, financial help, safety and security for our families, and other specific or timely needs. But in light of those requests, asking God for the reminder to see Him as our greatest and ultimate need above all. This looks like asking for His Word to fill us up, His promises to sustain us, and His presence to help us persevere. He promises to give us what we need for each day, as we seek first His kingdom and trust Him fully with our tomorrows (Matthew 25: 31-34).

As we enter into prayer and present our requests before God, asking Him to give us what we need for the day, we find confidence and comfort knowing our Father has invited us to go to Him and ask Him for our daily bread. Surely, He will not fail to supply what we need.

> We do not need great and frivolous riches, but we can come before God and ask Him for what we need, trusting that He will always give us whatever is required for life and godliness.

1. How does the theme of bread in John 6 and Exodus 16 help us to understand the petition to give us this day our daily bread?

2. Everything we have to sustain us through this life is a gift. In what ways does God provide for you on a day-to-day basis?

3. How can you depend physically and spiritually on God in a way that transforms your prayers and life?

FORGIVE US OUR DEBTS

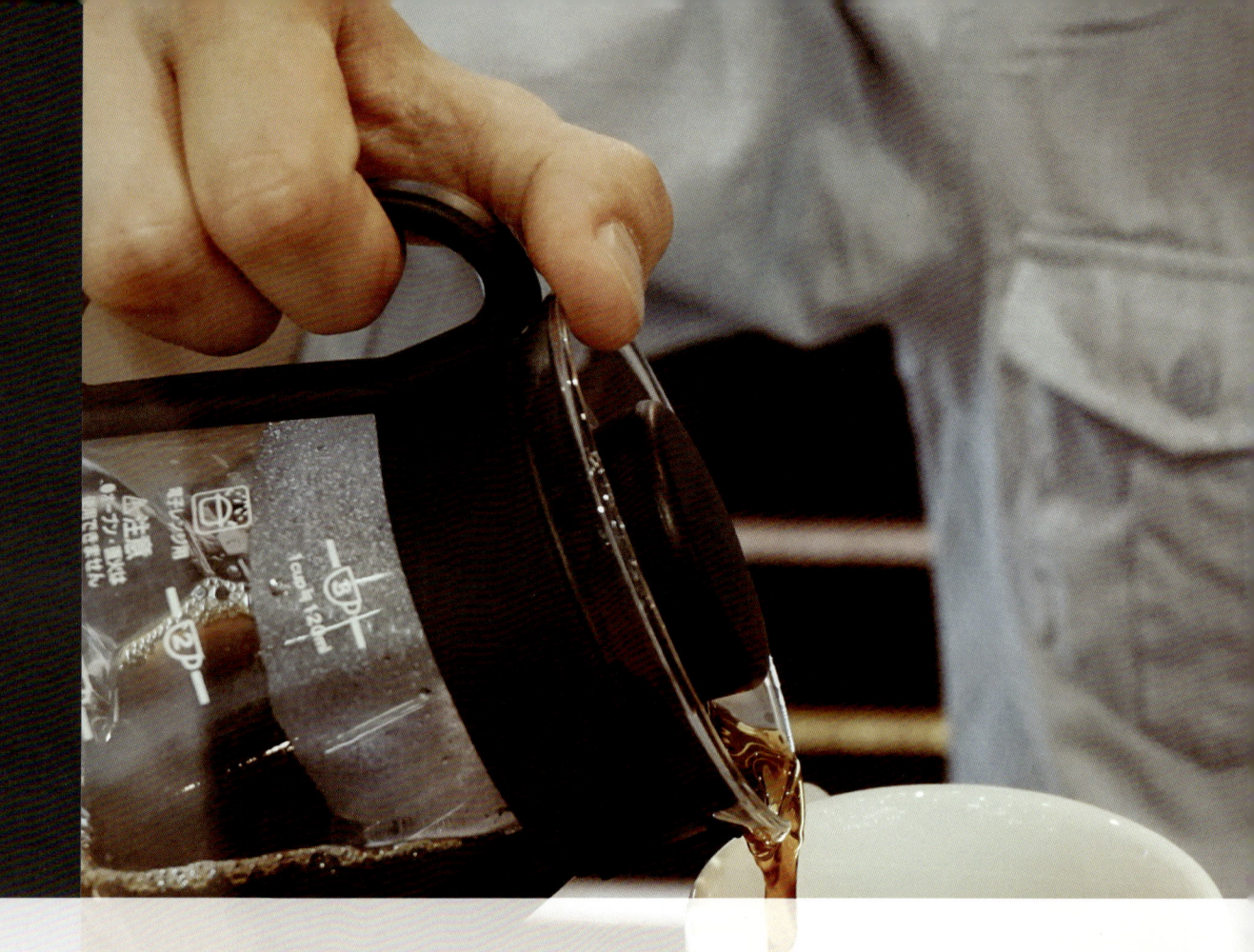

WEEK THREE

DAY 2

FORGIVE US OUR DEBTS AS WE ALSO HAVE FORGIVEN OUR DEBTORS

Read Matthew 6:12,
Ephesians 1:7,
1 John 1:9,
Colossians 3:12-13

When we think about debt, we might think about school loans, car payments, or credit card statements. Currently today, debt is a common annoyance, but in the ancient world, debt was punishable by a prison sentence. In the Roman Empire, prisons were mostly populated with debtors. If someone could not make good on their payments, they were incarcerated until they could pay what they owed. This system intended to put pressure on the families of those imprisoned for debt to pay up the debts of their loved ones so that they might be set free.

Jesus' use of the word debts is meant to draw our attention to the serious offense and punishment of impending debts. To be forgiven of debts is no small request but is a profound and merciful act. Yet, Jesus encourages His disciples to go to the Father and ask for forgiveness. The fifth petition of the Lord's Prayer is a plea that God would grant us forgiveness in order that we would have fellowship with God and fellowship with one another.

This petition in the Lord's Prayer reminds us of the gospel foundation of forgiveness. The basis for which we can even approach God in prayer is through the forgiveness that was offered to us in Christ Jesus. The ability to come near to God in prayer is a privilege and joy. But that privilege to commune freely with God came at a price. Because of our sin and disobedience, we were indebted to God and deserving of His wrath. Instead of leaving us to pay the penalty for our sin, God offered the forgiveness of sins through His one and only Son (Ephesians 1:7). Forgiveness is vital for fellowship with God. Although we have been fully and ultimately forgiven by God when we trust in Jesus as our Lord and Savior, we continue to seek immediate forgiveness by regularly repenting of our sin and asking God to forgive us. Sin is destructive, damaging, and hinders our relationship with God and others. We are called to continually repent and flee from all unrighteousness and God promises that when we do, in an ultimate and immediate sense, He is faithful and will forgive us (1 John 1:9).

Our immediate pursuits of repentance serve as an indicator of the ultimate forgiveness in Christ that we have already received. Because we love God and desire to obey Him, our disobedience should lead us to conviction, and our conviction to continual repentance. Asking God for forgiveness when we pray, reveals an unbending devotion to His commands and a humble recognition of the grace that He has offered us through Christ Jesus.

Understanding forgiveness offered to us in Christ should transform and shape how we forgive others. Just as forgiveness is vital to a relationship with God, forgiveness is essential to how we fellowship with others. Jesus is saying, as much as you have been forgiven, you ought to forgive others just as mercifully (Colossians 3:13). Pray for God to help you forgive freely. The forgiveness we show to others reflects true comprehension of God's forgiveness shown to us.

FORGIVENESS IS VITAL FOR FELLOWSHIP WITH GOD.

1. Describe in your own words the magnitude of forgiveness offered to you in Christ Jesus.

2. Although fully and ultimately forgiven, why should you seek immediate forgiveness from God in prayer?

3. What is the relationship between God's forgiveness to you and the forgiveness you show to others?

4. What effects have you seen from avoiding forgiveness and what fruit have you found in seeking forgiveness?

DO NOT BRING US INTO TEMPTATION

WEEK THREE

DAY 3

DO NOT BRING US INTO TEMPTATION

Read Matthew 6:13,
1 Peter 5:8,
James 1:12-16,
1 Corinthians 10:13

"It is only through the interceding of the Holy Spirit and the active work of God's Word in our hearts that we fight against temptation and sin."

Once laying a foundation for the disciples to confront their past sins in prayer, Jesus then directs their attention to how to approach the future temptations of sin in prayer. Temptation is relentless and no believer is exempt from it. We are daily faced with the temptation to sin, which can sometimes leave us feeling hopeless and defeated. But just as Jesus instructed his hearers to go to the Father and ask Him to not bring them to temptation, we are to do the same.

Does God lead us into temptation? What does Jesus really mean by these words? It is helpful to define the Greek term *peirasmos*, which is translated to mean temptation. In this context, the meaning of this term implies schemes of Satan or afflicting circumstances, neither of which we have sufficient strength or might to fight on our own to endure. The devil prowls around like a lion waiting for opportunities to lead us into temptation and to devour us (1 Peter 5:8). Sin and temptation are destructive. They are a real threat to our communion with God and the everyday life of a Christian. If we don't deal with temptation appropriately, it will give birth to sin, and Scripture tells us the sin leads to death (James 1:14-15).

We need God's help to refrain from falling into temptation. Even if we desire good, we are inclined toward evil. Our evil desires can tempt us to sin and ultimately lead us to destruction. We live in a constant state of spiritual warfare. We desire to do good, but we don't do it. (Romans 7:19) It is only through the interceding of the Holy Spirit and the active work of God's Word in our hearts that we fight against temptation and sin. Temptation in this life will come and we will not be able to fight against it on our own, but Jesus instructs His disciples to pray for protection and provision from the One who does have sufficient strength and power to prevail.

With God's help, trials can be used to refine us and shape us instead of destroying us. James 1:2-4 reminds us to, "Consider it a great joy, my brothers and sisters, whenever you experience various trials, because you know that the testing of your faith produces endurance. And let endurance have its full effect, so that you may be mature and complete, lacking nothing." How we respond to trials will determine whether we are tempted or tested. Although God does not tempt us (James 1:13), He can allow times of testing. For example, Jesus Himself was tested in the wilderness by Satan and overcame it (Matthew 4:1-11). In this case, God allowed testing, but God was not the instrument of temptation. When Jesus asks the Father to not bring us into temptation, He is modeling how His followers should pray knowing they are dependent on God to protect them from their evil desires that lead to sin.

God desires to make us holy as He is holy (1 Peter 1:16). He commands us to pursue righteousness and flee from sin. However, He does not issue the command without making a way. God promises that He will always provide a way for us to endure through trial (1 Corinthians 10:13). We are submitting to God's ultimate deliverance and pleading with God to spare us from the temptations and spiritual attacks of sin in everyday life. Jesus is teaching us to pray for endurance in the fight against temptation in the same way that we ask for daily bread. Sin and temptation will be a lifelong struggle, and we need the Lord for strength to overcome it. Daily pleading for God's protection from sin reveals a right understanding of the evils of this world and a right understanding of God's power and provision. We need the Lord's help to graciously guide us away from temptation at every turn.

> "Consider it a great joy, my brothers and sisters, whenever you experience various trials, because you know that the testing of your faith produces endurance. And let endurance have its full effect, so that you may be mature and complete, lacking nothing."
>
> JAMES 1:2-4

1. What does the battle against temptations look like in your life?

2. How does Scripture counsel you to endure through trials in this life?

3. How should knowing your own inclination towards sin spur you to daily pray against temptation?

DELIVER US FROM THE EVIL ONE

WEEK THREE

DAY 4

DELIVER US FROM THE EVIL ONE

Read Matthew 6:13,
1 John 5:19-20,
James 4:7,
Ephesians 6:10-17

"From beginning to end, the Bible tells the story of God's plan to deliver us from the evil one."

From beginning to end, the Bible tells the story of God's plan to deliver us from the evil one. In Genesis 3:15 we see the first glimpse of God's plan to crush the head of the serpent, Satan, the ultimate evil one who deceived Adam and Eve in the garden. Continuing through the Old Testament we see the promise of a seed through the line of Abraham (Genesis 26:3-5, Galatians 3:16), and the prophecy of a child in Isaiah (Isaiah 7:14). We see leaders like Moses (Dueteronomy 18:17-18) and kings like David (2 Samuel 7:12-13), pointing us towards a better king and a better leader. In the Gospels, this promise is born (Luke 2). This promise is Jesus Christ, the Savior of the world, our Rescuer, and our Deliverer. He lived among God's people, fully flesh and fully divine, knowing that the cross was set before Him. He died on the cross to pay the penalty for the sins of God's people. His resurrection defeated death once and for all and He assured deliverance from evil through His victory. While on the cross, Jesus' heel was bruised. But when He rose from the dead, Satan's head was crushed.

Our only hope in deliverance from evil is through Jesus Christ. We are incapable in and of ourselves. When we take on the righteousness of Christ, we put to death the desires of the flesh. In Christ, we share in His victorious defeat and we are supernaturally equipped to face the remaining evil of this world. We are prepared to wage war; strengthened by the Holy Spirit, putting on the full armor of God so that we might stand against the schemes of Satan (Ephesians 6:10-12). We are equipped with God's Word, which becomes a belt of truth around our waist to fight against deception and lies, and with righteousness as a shield (Ephesians 6:14). God fuels our faith to extinguish all the flaming arrows of the evil one (Ephesians 6:16).

We pray in hope that the Father would deliver us from evil now and forever. We live in both the already and not yet. He has already defeated sin. But we live waiting for this to be fully realized. Jesus teaches us to pray with urgency that God would deliver us from evil, and so we pray for the day when all will be made right in the world—when there will be no more pain, sorrow, sickness, or suffering, and evil will be defeated once and for all. As we wage war against sin and temptation, our anchor of hope is that God will help us now, and that victory is coming. We know that Satan is strong and more than capable of deception, but the stronger One has bound and defeated him. Jesus Christ wins the battle.

AND DO NOT BRING US INTO TEMPTATION, BUT DELIVER US FROM THE EVIL ONE.

1. How does God specifically equip us to face the evils of this world?

2. What is God doing now about evil? What will he do ultimately?

3. How can you ask God to deliver you from evil knowing that ultimate victory over evil awaits you in eternity?

FOR YOURS IS THE KINGDOM

WEEK THREE

DAY 5

72

FOR YOURS IS THE KINGDOM AND THE POWER AND THE GLORY. AMEN.

Read 1 Chronicles 29:11, Isaiah 42:8, Ephesians 1:19-21

Some of your translations may include, "For Yours is the kingdom and the power and the glory, forever and ever. Amen," in the Lord's Prayer. For other translations, this line is either not in the text or it is in brackets. This phrase has been recorded in a number of manuscripts; however, some translations have left it out because it is not found in the earliest manuscripts.

It was likely added in as a benediction in the early church as they used it for liturgical purposes. We find credence in its origin from 1 Chronicles 29:11. As David, the author of this prayer, attributed none of his successes to himself, the early church shared in this humble sentiment. Therefore, this benediction has and can continue to be uttered in full confidence of its theological accuracy; knowing that the point of this line is meant to position our hearts away from ourselves and toward the kingdom, power, and glory of our wonderful God.

In the New Testament, benedictions were often given at the close of a service or written at the end of a letter. The benedictions were often biblical passages written in the form of blessing and encouragement given to the brothers and sisters in the church (Ephesians 6:23-24), praise and worship to God (Ephesians 3:20-21), or invoking love and full trinitarian work in (2 Corinthians 13:13). Each reference of a benediction is placed at the end of a teaching or prayer to reorient our hearts from what we speak about to who we speak to. It is intended to offer up a final, all-encompassing, blessing. Our prayers, whether in word or thought, should be shaped by this same principle. Using this benediction at the closing of the Lord's Prayer allows a response that draws attention to all that God is and all that God has done. We close this prayer with a heart, mind and soul that exclaims, "It's all Yours, Lord. You are worthy of it all. In all these things, may You receive all the glory and praise."

We pray and ask God with expectation and hope that God will accomplish all of His purposes (Isaiah 46:9-11). Saying "Amen" is a proclamation of our faith and an affirmation of God's ultimate and final reign and rule. This is to be our final word at the end of our prayers, meaning "so it be." We sow and we sleep, trusting Him with the ultimate results of all of our faith-filled utterances. Our requests remind us of our humanity while our amens remind us of God's divinity. May our prayers conclude with a heart that believes in this truth as easily as we speak this small word. So, it be, Lord.

The entirety of the Lord's Prayer models how we as Christians ought to approach a holy God; as needy creatures in need of grace—grace for daily bread, grace for forgiveness, grace for protection, and grace to behold the beauty of God's glory. As is the way for needy creatures, Christians ask, but our asking is always filled with hope. God, who offered up His own Son for our sake, will always graciously give His people all that we need for life and godliness (Romans 8:32). He abounds in grace and overflows with care. And therefore, we can confidently leave our prayers in the gracious hands of the God who cares for us without measure. To Him be the glory and honor forever and ever. Amen.

> We close this prayer with a heart, mind and soul that exclaims, "It's all Yours, Lord. You are worthy of it all. In all these things, may You receive all the glory and praise."

1. How does a recognition of the ultimate reign of God anchor our hope in prayer?

2. After reading Ephesians 1:19-21, what confidence do you have in God's power and authority when you approach Him in prayer?

3. How can you intentionally conclude your prayers by giving utmost praise and glory to God? How will you practically implement this in your prayer life?

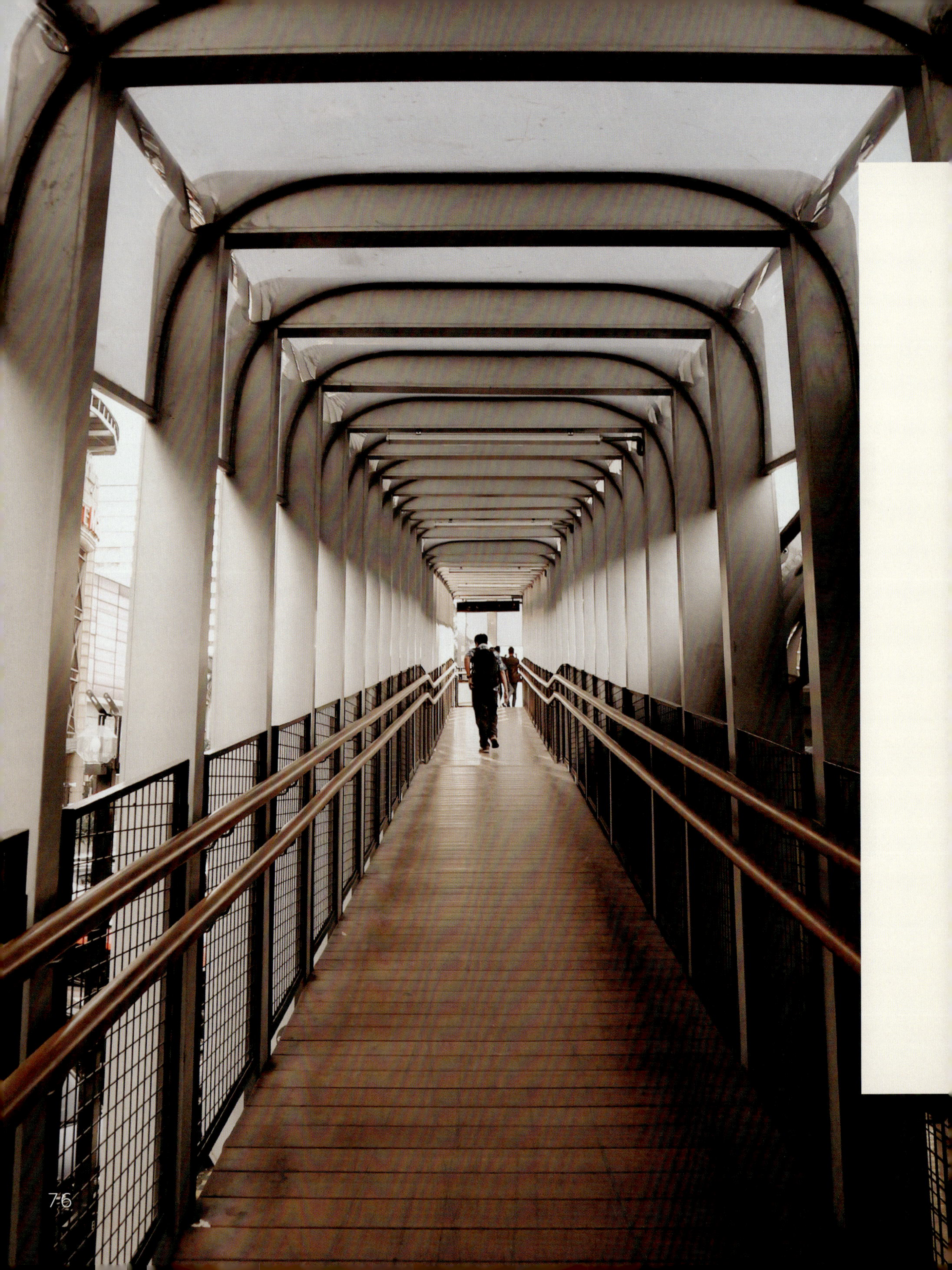

GIVE US TODAY OUR DAILY BREAD. AND FORGIVE US OUR DEBTS, AS WE ALSO HAVE FORGIVEN OUR DEBTORS. AND DO NOT BRING US INTO TEMPTATION, BUT DELIVER US FROM THE EVIL ONE.

MATTHEW 6:11-13

WEEKLY REFLECTION

Week Three: Review all passages from the week

Paraphrase the passages from this week.

What did you observe from this week's text about God and His character?

What do these passages teach about the condition of mankind and about yourself?

How do these passage point to the gospel?

How should you respond to these passages? What is the personal application?

What specific action steps can you take this week to apply these passages?

BENEDICTIONS IN SCRIPTURE

Consider these passages of Scripture and how you can incorporate them into your prayers. As we concluded in the study, benedictions in prayer offer final, all-encompassing praise to God. Take a passage, memorize it, and practice actively praying that Scripture into your prayers.

ROMANS 15:13

Now may the God of hope fill you with all joy and peace as you believe so that you may overflow with hope by the power of the Holy Spirit.

EPHESIANS 3:20-21

Now to him who is able to do above and beyond all that we ask or think according to the power that works in us—to him be glory in the church and in Christ Jesus to all generations, forever and ever. Amen.

PHILIPPIANS 4:7

And the peace of God, which surpasses all understanding, will guard your hearts and minds in Christ Jesus.

1 TIMOTHY 1:17

Now to the King eternal, immortal, invisible, the only God, be honor and glory forever and ever. Amen.

1 TIMOTHY 6:15-16

God will bring this about in his own time. He is the blessed and only Sovereign, the King of kings, and the Lord of lords, who alone is immortal and who lives in unapproachable light, whom no one has seen or can see, to him be honor and eternal power. Amen.

HEBREWS 13:20-21

Now may the God of peace, who brought up from the dead our Lord Jesus—the great Shepherd of the sheep—through the blood of the everlasting covenant, equip you with everything good to do his will, working in us what is pleasing in his sight, through Jesus Christ, to whom be glory forever and ever. Amen.

2 JOHN 1:3

Grace, mercy, and peace will be with us from God the Father and from Jesus Christ, the Son of the Father, in truth and love.

JUDE 1:24-25

Now to him who is able to protect you from stumbling and to make you stand in the presence of his glory, without blemish and with great joy, to the only God our Savior, through Jesus Christ our Lord, be glory, majesty, power, and authority before all time, now and forever. Amen.

REVELATION 5:12B, 13B

Worthy is the Lamb who was slaughtered to receive power and riches and wisdom and strength and honor and glory and blessing! I heard every creature in heaven, on earth, under the earth, on the sea, and everything in them say, Blessing and honor and glory and power be to the one seated on the throne, and to the Lamb, forever and ever!"

REVELATION 22:20-21

He who testifies about these things says, "Yes, I am coming soon." Amen! Come, Lord Jesus! The grace of the Lord Jesus be with everyone. Amen."

PETITIONS OF THE LORD'S PRAYER

GOD-CENTERED	NEED-CENTERED
Praying for God's name to be honored as holy	Praying for daily needs (spiritual + physical)
Praying for God's Kingdom to come	Praying for forgiveness and a forgiving spirit
Praying for God's will to be done	Praying to be lead away from temptation and delivered from evil

31 DAYS OF PRAYER

Practice the implications of this study and incorporate specific prayer prompts daily for 31 days. Some of these prompts may not be specific to you (i.e. spouse, children, new baby, co-workers, boss, etc.). Use them as an opportunity to pray for someone else or to pray that God would fulfill the desires of your heart for them.

1. Spouse
2. Children
3. Parents
4. Neighbors
5. Your city
6. Co-workers
7. Your boss
8. A friend that lives close
9. A long-distance friend
10. Grieving friend or family
11. A newlywed couple
12. A new baby
13. Siblings
14. Grandparents
15. A widow
16. A new believer
17. A non-christian
18. A member of your extended family
19. A Church family member
20. Your Pastor
21. Your elders
22. Your church
23. A missionary
24. The president
25. Your city officials
26. Your state officials
27. Your community helpers: firefighters, police officers, medical professionals, and teachers
28. A specific ministry
29. Delight in God's Word
30. Boldness with the gospel
31. For sanctification and perseverance in the faith

WHAT IS THE GOSPEL?

Thank you for reading and enjoying this study with us!

We are abundantly grateful for the Word of God, the instruction we glean from it, and the ever-growing understanding about God's character from it. We're also thankful that Scripture continually points to one thing in innumerable ways: the gospel.

We remember our brokenness when we read about the fall of Adam and Eve in the garden of Eden (Genesis 3), when sin entered into a perfect world and maimed it. We remember the necessity that something innocent must die to pay for our sin when we read about the atoning sacrifices in the Old Testament. We read that we have all sinned and fallen short of the glory of God (Romans 3:23), and that the penalty for our brokenness, the wages of our sin, is death (Romans 6:23). We all are in need of grace and mercy, but most importantly, we all need a Savior.

We consider the goodness of God when we realize that He did not plan to leave us in this dire state. We see His promise to buy us back from the clutches of sin and death in Genesis 3:15. And we see that promise accomplished with Jesus Christ on the cross. Jesus Christ knew no sin yet became sin so that we might become righteous through His sacrifice (2 Corinthians 5:21). Jesus was tempted in every way that we are and lived sinlessly. He was reviled, yet still yielded Himself for our sake, that we may have life abundant in Him. Jesus lived the perfect life that we could not live, and died the death that we deserved.

The gospel is profound yet simple. There are many mysteries in it that we can never exhaust this side of heaven, but there is still overwhelming weight to its implications in this life. The gospel is the telling of our sinfulness and God's goodness, and this gracious gift compels a response. We are saved by grace through faith, which means that we rest with faith in the grace that Jesus Christ displayed on the cross (Ephesians 2:9). We cannot save ourselves from our brokenness or do any amount of good works to merit God's favor, but we can have faith that what Jesus accomplished in His death, burial, and resurrection was more than enough for our salvation and our eternal delight. When we accept God, we are commanded to die to our self and our sinful desires, and live a life worthy of the calling we've received (Ephesians 4:1). The gospel compels us to be sanctified, and in so doing, we are conformed to the likeness of Christ Himself. This is hope. This is redemption. This is the gospel.

THANK YOU

for studying God's Word with us

CONNECT WITH US

@THEDAILYGRACECO
@KRISTINSCHMUCKER

CONTACT US

INFO@THEDAILYGRACECO.COM

SHARE

#THEDAILYGRACECO
#LAMPANDLIGHT

VISIT US ONLINE

THEDAILYGRACECO.COM

MORE DAILY GRACE

THE DAILY GRACE APP
DAILY GRACE PODCAST